PEPERONI BOOKS

Photographs and Text
by Michael Kerstgens

COAL NOT DOLE

The Miners' Strike 1984 / 1985

To Mariele, Paul, Robert, and Klara.
To my friends and family.

Contents

Imprint

I was right at the beginning of my studies and had only just begun to explore the medium of photography. Looking back, I now see that I was really in search of myself and – under the recent influence of the photographer and filmmaker Robert Frank – an appropriate subject matter. I had good contacts in Wales, where my godfather, Hermann Heinrich, was managing director of Thyssen-Schachtbau Great Britain Ltd. As a 16-year-old, I had already done six weeks of work experience at Thyssen. I therefore imagined it would all be very easy. This, I soon realised, was naïve.

In preparation for my trip, I had attended a benefit event of IG-Bergbau, the German equivalent of the National Union of Mineworkers, at the – appropriately enough – decommissioned Carl Colliery in Essen. The UK miners' strike was already eight months old. I spoke with a NUM representative who was there to take receipt of donations and declarations of solidarity with the striking miners. Various actors from *Rote Erde*, a highly acclaimed TV drama series on coal mining in the Ruhr, had also been invited. When I told the NUM representative of my plan, he said that if I wanted to photograph the strike, I would need to be clear about which side I was on. His words were plain and spoke volumes about the role played by the British media during the 12 months of industrial action.

As it happened, Hermann Heinrich was unable to help. Companies supplying the UK mining industry, including Thyssen-Schachtbau, had also been badly affected by the industrial action. My godfather was sympathetic towards the miners and their predicament but not towards the union representing them. For a while, many ancillary firms were forced to work short time, which only increased their frustration at the NUM and its president, Arthur Scargill, strike leader and chief political adversary of Prime Minister Margaret Thatcher. Thyssen-Schachtbau was already moving into new areas of business, but mining still remained a big part of the company portfolio.

The strike was brutal and tore a rift through British society, entire mining communities, and even individual families. I took photographs at several children's Christmas parties – funded by German unions – and visited a number of pits in the Welsh valleys, where the pithead buildings looked more like churches. I also met representatives of German unions, who had brought presents for the children of strikebound mining communities along with money and moral support for their parents.

Yet there was little or no contact to the striking miners themselves. And, when there was, they were still wary of me, as a German. Moreover, they all knew where I was from, since Thyssen workers, acting with the best intentions, had told them to expect me. Many of the miners at Cynheidre Colliery – which had been the scene of a serious accident, with six deaths, in 1971 – still remembered my father, Alfred, who worked for Thyssen-Schachtbau from 1953 to 1965. That was nice but, if anything, a hindrance to my work. Frustrated at the lack of opportunities to take photographs, I resolved to leave Wales and travel to the heart of the strike in Yorkshire.

A childhood friend by the name of Uwe Gramann – whose father, Otto, had likewise gone to Wales in the early 1950s – was now serving in the Llanelli police force. He lent me his VW dormobile to drive to Barnsley in South Yorkshire.

It was Boxing Day when I arrived, the weather bitterly cold, and I spent the first night in the van. The next morning, I stood outside the locked doors of the NUM office. The address and telephone number had been given to me by the NUM representative I had met in Essen. Located in the same building was a strike helpline, where a kind-hearted counsellor gave me sanctuary for a couple of hours. Over sandwiches and piping-hot tea, he began to tell me about some of the problems faced by the striking miners. Several hours later, the door swung open to reveal a man by the name of Stuart Marshall – small, stocky, and covered in tattoos. Call me "Spud", he said.

Having listened to my story, he promptly invited me back to stay with his family. Spud and his wife, Marsha, her son, Mark, daughter, Jill, and Jill's boyfriend, Tony "Clip" Carlton, all lived in the row of small terraced houses on Rimington Road, in Wombwell, near Barnsley. From the window, you could see the strikebound Darfield Main Colliery, the shaft of which was sunk in 1861. Clip was a steelworker and had come out on strike in sympathy with the miners. So it was that I landed right in the middle of one of the most bitter industrial conflicts that the UK has ever seen.

It was agreed that I could stay for as long as I liked, accompany them wherever they went, and, most important of all, take photographs.

There was only one condition: "You buy the veg!" That was the deal – or so I thought. So I bought vegetables whenever I could. It was only later that I realised they were just pulling my leg.

After a while, I stopped buying carrots and, instead, was expected to pay my turn at the bar of Wombwell Working Men's Club on Station Road. It was often a big round, which added considerably to the expenses of my trip. But I was glad to pay and, in return, got to hear some rare jokes about the "Krauts", as the Germans were still known in the UK. It was a magical time and I often ended the evening drunk, much to the amusement of my companions.

Spud was a miner in the fourth generation and worked at Darfield Main Colliery. Before the strike, Marsha Marshall had been a house-wife and essentially apolitical in her views. Following Spud's first arrest, however, she rose to become one of the leading lights of Woman Against Pit Closures (WAPC). As spokeswoman of the Barnsley group, she was often seen on television and regularly received calls from the British actress and political activist Vanessa Redgrave. She was an impressive figure and a rousing speaker.

Thanks to Spud and Marsha, I was able to photograph meetings and rallies to which the press would never have been invited. Spud introduced me to the rest of the striking miners with the words:

"This is Michael. He's from Germany, and he's a mate."

That was how I came to meet the NUM leader, Arthur Scargill, for whom Spud sometimes acted as a bodyguard and driver.

While the men were the spearhead of the strike movement, the WAPC formed its heart. Contrary to popular belief, the women weren't restricted to working in the soup kitchens. In fact, I saw lots of miners doing duties in the makeshift kitchens, while their womenfolk were busy elsewhere, organising rallies and holding firebrand speeches. Some of the women travelled right around the world, collecting support and donations. It was this radicalism, rigorous and pure, that impressed me more than anything.

Unlike the political radicalism of Scargill, who would remain a lifelong supporter of the Communist Party, the radicalism I experienced here was deeply rooted within the very traditions of the mining industry and the mining community. People here knew where they came from, and they were proud of it.

It was a radical and proletarian consciousness, quite unlike the social-democratic folklore that I had already began to notice back home in the Ruhr area. It was, for example, completely at odds with the romanticised picture of mining presented in Klaus Emmerich's nine-part TV drama series *Rote Erde* in 1983. Seldom have I witnessed such a deep and powerful sense of tradition, there in the UK, during the last great labour struggle of British industrial history. The strike marked the end of the mining era in Britain, and it ended in bitter defeat for the miners. Entire communities disappeared from the map – and, with them, a tradition of coal mining that had spanned generations. On top of the loss of their livelihood and a wage of, on average, £9,000 a year, many of the striking miners ran up debts of around £10,000 – money borrowed to tide over their families during the strike. Many of them went short of food, and many were utterly demoralised.

There was huge pressure within the mining communities to continue strike action, but more and more proved unequal to the challenge, and the solidarity on the picket line began to crumble. At the end of 12 months, the strike collapsed.

All in all, 70,000 miners would lose their job. The end of the miners' strike marked the beginning of an era of neoliberal politics in which nationalised industries were privatised with the sole aim of maximising profits. It was the birth of deregulation, the chief tenets of which were laid down in the 1980s by conservatives such as Margaret Thatcher, US President Ronald Reagan, and German Chancellor Helmut Kohl, followed by Tony Blair's New Labour and Gerhard Schröder's Social Democracy in the 1990s.

A website dedicated to the late Margaret Thatcher has the following to say: "The one-year strike of 1984 marked the last gasp of the old union system. Since then, Great Britain has not witnessed another major industrial dispute."

On 3rd January 2014, *The Guardian* revealed a secret plan to use the army at the height of the miners' strike. As the online article explained, cabinet papers released to the National Archives show that the Thatcher government had made preparations to use troops to move coal to power stations.

What interested me then was not the political significance but rather the social dimension of the strike and the lives of the families involved. To convey some sense of the strike and its aftermath, it must be remembered that when industrial action began, there were over 170 working mines in the UK with more than 180,000 employees.

Behind this figure lie countless stories of the families and communities involved. By 2004, there were only 15 pits and fewer than 7,000 people working in the coal industry. The defeat had a devastating impact on the mining communities. A study published in 2005 by the Centre for Regional Economic and Social Research at Sheffield Hallam University investigated economic and social change in the English and Welsh coalfields over the period from 1981 to 2004.

It concluded that after 20 years, despite a certain degree of economic recovery, only around 60 percent of the jobs lost in the UK coal industry had been replaced. That still left 90,000 coal jobs that had vanished without trace. The authors argued that even in a favourable climate, it would probably take a dozen years or more for Britain's coalfields to catch up with the rest of the economy. In Britain's coalfields, the proportion of "economically inactive" men of working age was above the national average, and estimates put the figure for the "hidden unemployed" as high as 100,000 men. *

As a farewell present, Spud presented me with a miner's lamp, a trophy for the Fire Fighting Competition of 1983, and a pint glass upon which he had engraved his name and everyone else's along with the dedication:

"To Michael – Hands across the water, Hands across the sea".

For the "Germans" in Llanelli, the strike had but a limited impact, since most of them were close to retirement anyway. Only a few have since returned to Germany, and some are now buried in Wales. The Llanelli headquarters of Thyssen Great Britain Ltd. closed at the end of the 1980s. As for Cynheidre Colliery, the coal mine which my father helped to set up in the years from 1953 to 1965, there is nothing left now but a fence.

* "Twenty years on: has the economy of the coalfields recovered?" (2005), Beatty, Fothergill, and Powell, Centre for Regional Economic and Social Research, Sheffield Hallam University

1984

Photographs
South Wales

Children's Christmas party
Working Men's and Social Club
Llanelli, South Wales, 1984

Children's Christmas party
Working Men's and Social Club
Llanelli, South Wales, 1984

NUM Office at Cynheidre Colliery
Llanelli, South Wales, 1984

Near Kiveton Park Colliery, 1984

Backyards in Rimington Road
Wombwell, 1984

Smith Street/Station Road
Wombwell, 1984

Backyards
Kiveton Park, 1984

A miner watches an interview with
NUM President Arthur Scargill
Wombwell, 1984

Jill, daughter of WAPC activist Marsha Marshall, lives with
her boyfriend, Clip Carlton, and daughter, Carla
Rimington Road, Wombwell, 1984

Smith Street, Wombwell, 1984

In the kitchen, Spud tattoos a young miner
Rimington Road, Wombwell, 1985

News on the next day's picketing
Rimington Road, Wombwell, 1985

Spud Marshall with grandchild Carla
Rimington Road, Wombwell, 1985

Coal Picking

UK miners were allocated a coal allowance with which to heat their homes – as was also traditional in the German coal industry. During the strike, the National Coal Board (NCB) stopped deliveries to striking miners. They were therefore forced to go coal picking on old spoil heaps. The low-grade coal had a poor heating value and, due to the high stone content and other debris, produced palls of thick smoke that hung above the houses. It was not uncommon to see whole families picking for coal. Those with a retired miner in the family continued to receive a coal allowance and were able to share some of this around.

There were numerous accidents. Particularly tragic was the death of three teenage boys while picking coal in Goldthorpe, South Yorkshire, on 11th November 1984.

Striking miners picking coal on a spoil heap
Elsecar, South Yorkshire, 1984

Kiveton Park Colliery (closed 1994)
South Yorkshire, 1984

Retired miner picking coal on a spoil heap
at Kiveton Park Colliery
South Yorkshire, 1984

Striking miners picking coal on a spoil heap
Elsecar, South Yorkshire, 1984

Chimneys smoking from low-grade coal
South Yorkshire, 1984

Woman Against Pit Closures (WAPC)

The wives and partners of the miners became organised in a movement known as Woman Against Pit Closures (WAPC). This not only played a key role in the strike itself but also changed the role of women in the male-dominated world of mining. Feminists from around the world came to the UK to support the women of the WAPC. The movement originated in Barnsley, South Yorkshire, where the first WAPC group was formed in March 1984. On 11th August 1984, a national WAPC march was held in London. Attended by 23,000 women from throughout the UK, it ensured that the movement became known worldwide. Some of the WAPC activists travelled abroad to ask for support and donations.

Marsha Marshall, secretary of the WAPC Barnsley group, travelled to France, Italy, Bulgaria, and the USSR. She had never been abroad before. In Rome, she spoke to a rally of 4,000 Italian trade unionists.

A meeting of the Barnsley group of the WAPC
Barnsley, December 1984

WAPC activists Marsha Marshall and Anne Scargill
at a meeting in Barnsley, December 1984

A meeting of the Barnsley group of the WAPC
Barnsley, December 1984

WAPC picketing with NUM President Arthur Scargill (3rd from right)
New Year's Day picket at the Ferrybridge coal-fired power station West
Yorkshire, 1985

WAPC activist Betty Cook with NUM President Arthur Scargill on the New Year's Day picket at the Ferrybridge coal-fired power station West Yorkshire, 1985

WAPC activist Marsha Marshall (left) and daughter Jill (with boyfriend Clip and
daughter Carla) watch a BBC interview with Marsha
Rimington Road, Wombwell, 1985

WAPC activist Marsha Marshall supports
picketing miners with a donation of cigarettes
South Yorkshire, December 1984

AT THIS MEETING I WANT TO SAY HOW WE HAVE TO CARRY ON OUR FIGHT AGAINST MRS THATCHER, AND HER HIT MAN NAMELY MR. McGREGOR, WHO IS DETERMINED TO CLOSE DOWN OUR PITS. IF HE GETS AWAY WITH IT THERE WILL BE NO STOPPING HIM. AND LET'S BEAR IN MIND WHO THIS MAN IS, HE'S A YANK, TELLING OUR HUSBAND'S AND SON'S WHO ARE BRITISH BORN AND BRED THERE IS NO FUTURE IN THE COAL INDUSTRY FOR YOU. B·S·C HAD TO BE CUT AND GOD KNOW'S HOW MANY MORE. THIS IS THE REASON FOR VAST UNEMPLOYMENT. AND IT WILL ESCULATE IN THE VERY NEAR FUTURE. WE ARE NOT NEAR A SETTLEMENT, BUT THE FIGHT TO OPPOSE PIT CLOSURES IS WELL OF THE GROUND, WE HAVE

THE BACKING OF THE N·U·R, THE SEAMEN AND ASLEF, THEY REALISE WHAT THIS FIGHT MEANS. COAL IS A VITAL RESOURCE OF THIS COUNTRY NOT ONLY TO MINER'S BUT TO OTHER INDUSTRIES ASWELL. THIS IS WHY THEY ARE GIVING THEIR SUPPORT IN BACKING THE MINERS, AND BY BLACKING MOVEMENTS OF COAL. IF WE GOT ALL THE BACKING OF ALL N·U·M. MEMBER'S OUR FIGHT WOULD BE TAKEN MORE SERIOUSLY, AND THE BRITISH PEOPLE WOULD THEN KNOW HOW SERIOUS THE SITUATION IS. THE MINER'S HAVE TO WIN THIS FIGHT, IF THEY DON'T THEIR FUTURE WILL BE AS BLACK AS COAL ITSELF, AND THE WEEKLY WAGE PACKET WILL BE A GIRO - HANDOUT, AND AS ALL YOU KNOW THAT IS THE END OF THE ROAD.

"... their future will be as black as coal itself,
and the weekly wage packet will be a giro-handout ..."

Marsha Marshall at the beginning of the strike, 1984

WAPC activist Marsha Marshall
telephones with Vanessa Redgrave
Rimington Road, Wombwell, 1985

WAPC Soup Kitchens

Times were exceptionally hard for all of the miners during the strike. With its assets frozen, the NUM was unable to pay strike relief to its members. Many had to remortgage their homes or live from savings. Some received support from a NUM relief fund that was financed by donations from abroad, including the former Eastern Block.

The soup kitchens operated on the strength of contributions by members of the public, local supermarkets, farmers, and church organisations. People from throughout the UK travelled to the coalfields to donate food. Families without any money at all could go to the soup kitchens to get a warm meal and a packed lunch for their children. The soup kitchens were organised by the women from the WAPC and by social and welfare clubs.

WAPC soup kitchen
Mitchell & Darfield Social Club
Roy Kilner Road, Wombwell, 1985

WAPC soup kitchen
Mitchell & Darfield Social Club
Roy Kilner Road, Wombwell, 1985

WAPC soup kitchen
Mitchell & Darfield Social Club
Roy Kilner Road, Wombwell, 1985

WAPC soup kitchen
Mitchell & Darfield Social Club
Roy Kilner Road, Wombwell, 1985

Darfield Main Branch Meeting

NUM branch meetings brought together miners from one or a number of collieries. Such gatherings were an opportunity to discuss strike action, picketing, major rallies, and the state of negotiations with the National Coal Board (NCB) and the British government. The meetings were restricted to striking miners, and only they knew exactly when they would take place. As a rule, they were held in the local social club.

On 5th January 1985, local NUM officials called an official branch meeting for Darfield Main Colliery at the Mitchell & Darfield Social Club in Wombwell. Following 10 months of strike action, the mood was deeply depressed.

NUM branch meeting for Darfield Main Colliery
at Mitchell & Darfield Social Club
Roy Kilner Road, Wombwell, 5th January 1985

NUM branch meeting for Darfield Main Colliery
at Mitchell & Darfield Social Club
Roy Kilner Road, Wombwell, 5th January 1985

A NUM official adresses the branch meeting
at Mitchell & Darfield Social Club
Roy Kilner Road, Wombwell, 5th January 1985

NUM branch meeting for Darfield Main Colliery
at Mitchell & Darfield Social Club
Roy Kilner Road, Wombwell, 5th January 1985

Working Men's Social Club

The first working men's social and welfare clubs were established in England around 1865. They were created for educational and recreational purposes and continue to play an important role in working-class communities in the former industrial heartlands of the UK. A working men's club is usually equipped with a bar and a function room. Its facilities can be used for political and union-related meetings as well as social, music, wedding, and anniversary functions.

Mitchell & Darfield Social Club
Roy Kilner Road, Wombwell, 1985

Function room of Wombwell Working Men's Club
Station Road, Wombwell, 1984

Social at Wombwell Working Men's Club
Station Road, Wombwell, 1984

New Year's Eve with neighbours and friends
at Wombwell Working Men's Club
Station Road, Wombwell, 1984

New Year's Eve Spud and Mark help
a reveller make his way home
Wombwell, 1985

A Wombwell pub, 1985

Joyce and Derek in a Wombwell pub, 1985

Picket Lines

Picketing was organised by the NUM and on a local level by the miners themselves. Miners not only picketed their own place of work but also joined forces to form so-called flying pickets – highly mobile units that would travel to pits in neighbouring regions Nobody quite knew when and where flying pickets would appear. They were feared by the authorities, since the police were often at a loss to predict the precise scale of a protest.

The British government reacted with an unprecedented crackdown. Special police units, some of them mounted, were deployed against the striking miners. Over the 12 months of the strike, 11 people died and 9,000 were injured, including many police officers. During the same period, 11,000* miners were arrested. The scenes of violence at the mass pickets at Cortonwood and Orgreave would divide public opinion for years to come.

* The figures cited above vary widely according to their origin and tend to be higher in sources to the left of the political spectrum than in press and other publicly accessible archives.

Every morning, a game of cat and mouse
between the police and flying pickets
South Yorkshire, 1985

Spud Marshall on a picket line
at the Cortonwood Colliery
South Yorkshire, 1985

Police attempt to prevent miners picketing
access to Cortonwood Colliery
South Yorkshire, 1985

All in all, some 9,000 striking miners were
injured during the course of the one-year strike
Cortonwood, South Yorkshire, 1985

28 Years Later

Spud Marshall

Spud Marshall at Wombwell Working Men's Club
Station Road, Wombwell, September 2012

Spud Marshall at home in Kendray
Barnsley, September 2012

Poundland

By Michael Kerstgens

The headquarters of the National Union of Mineworkers is on Barnsley's Huddersfield Road. The political and social clout once wielded by the miners' union has long since waned. With membership dwindling, NUM meetings are no longer the militant occasions they were in the days of the strike. In the local working men's clubs, the years of struggle, resignation, and, ultimately, despair are etched like deep scars into the faces of former miners. Nobody wants to hear about Arthur Scargill anymore at the NUM, where all traces of his former presidency have been erased. Following a legal dispute in 2012 about unauthorised union payments for a London flat, he is now persona non grata. Instead, the most visible testament to the glory days are the proud banners of collieries past and present – silent witnesses to a bygone, heroic age of mining – that hang in the headquarters' imposing assembly hall.

On the streets outside, banners of a different kind tell of another struggle: "short-term loans", "for sale", and "buy one, get one free" are the slogans of a region seemingly up for sale. Society splits into those with money to spend and those without, those in work and those on the dole. Youth unemployment has more than doubled over the last two years in Barnsley, where long-term unemployment for 16–24-year-olds is among the worst in the UK. For every job advertised in this age group, there are 15 potential applicants. With Britain caught in the grip of a recession, the Barnsley and Dearne Valley area has been especially badly hit.

Almost 25 percent of families here live below the official poverty line. As Sean McGuire, chief executive of Ambitious Minds, explains: "Those areas which have suffered disproportionately in the last five years need support to prevent unemployment, and especially long-term unemployment, becoming normalised." As ever, the government of the day carefully massages the figures. "The real level of unemployment 2012", a study by the Centre for Regional Economic and Social Research at Sheffield Hallam University, shows that the official statistics mask the true number of people out of work. For example, they fail to reflect the amount of hidden unemployed – those fit for work but receiving some form of benefit while participating in one of a number of schemes. These include training courses for school-leavers, who thereby disappear from the official figures, and programmes for those fit for work but currently not actively seeking a job for health-related or other reasons.

Meanwhile, in the world of globalised commerce, the multinationals wage a relentless campaign in pursuit of greater market share, without a thought for local ties or tradition. The result is a ferocious battle over scant incomes – and an increasingly beleaguered high street unable to hold its own against the big supermarket chains. There is little to provide a sense of belonging, as the unions once did. Once upon a time, jobs were handed down from generation to generation; today, the enduring legacy is unemployment.

As Marsha Marshall foretold in one of her speeches 30 years ago, it all looks very much like "the end of the road".

Assembly hall at the NUM headquarters
Huddersfield Road, Barnsley, 2013

Assembly hall at the
NUM headquarters
Huddersfield Road,
Barnsley 2013

Assembly hall at the NUM headquarters
Huddersfield Road, Barnsley, 2013

Assembly hall at the NUM headquarters
Huddersfield Road, Barnsley, 2013

Mitchell & Darfield Social Club
Wombwell

Phil Briscoe and Spud Marshall were both miners at the Darfield
Main Colliery in Wombwell. Phil was a miner from 1970 until the
colliery was closed in 1989. Since 1997, he has been working as a club
steward at the Mitchell & Darfield Social Club.

Before long, they are harking back to the old times down the pit,
the backbreaking work, and, of course, the miners' strike and its
consequences. The club is empty. Only a few of their old workmates
still call by. So few, in fact, that the club now shuts in the afternoon.
In the evening, there are dances and bingo.

For Spud, it's the first time in years he's been back to the club. "It's
like a graveyard in here," he says. Nevertheless, there's still a real
warmth between the two former comrades-in-arms.

Spud Marshall at the
Mitchell & Darfield Social Club
Wombwell, 2013

Rimington Road, Wombwell, 2013

Rimington Road, Wombwell, 2013

Rimington Road, Wombwell, 2013

Working Men's Club,
Station Road, Wombwell, 2013

High Street, Wombwell, 2013

Lavender Court, Barnsley

Spud Marshall now lives in Kendray, another part of Barnsley. He and Marsha sold their house in Wombwell back in 2006. Faced with Marsha's illness, they had no option but to move into a form of sheltered accommodation. People from the neighbourhood still come to him for tattoos, just as they did 30 years ago. He knows that his clients, most of them unemployed, don't have much spare cash, so he only charges a pound for a loved one's name or a fiver at most for a decorative image. They can also be sure of a sympathetic ear to their problems.

Carl, aged 23, is sitting in Spud's kitchen. He has come to get a tattoo of the name of his five-month-old son, Blake. He and his girlfriend Roxanne have been out of work since leaving school at the age of 16 and have just £600 to live on each month. Their daughter, Tina-Marie, is five years old.

Lavender Court, Barnsley, 2013

Barnsley, 2013

Word of Thanks

I would like to express my thanks to my admirable godfather, Hermann Heinrich, to his Welsh wife, Lynne, to their family, and to Uwe Gramann, who today lives in New Zealand. Back in 1984, they helped me stand on my own two feet and gave me the confidence to travel to Yorkshire. Hermann and I met up in South Wales as recently as 2009 and talked about the events of that period. Born in Liegnitz in Silesia in 1923, he passed away in 2011 at the age of 87.

An immense debt of gratitude is owed also to Marsha and Stuart "Spud" Marshall, to their family and friends in Wombwell, and to all the striking miners who showed so much faith in me during the winter of 1984/85. Today, I know that Spud, Marsha, and the rest of the mining families in South Yorkshire never entirely got over the crushing defeat of the strike and its aftermath. In the subsequent period, Marsha fell seriously ill. I am truly grateful to both of them for their help during my stay and for the friendship they showed me.

In 2009, following a long illness, Marsha Marshall died at the age of 64 in Barnsley, where her husband, and my friend, Spud, still lives.

For support and help:

Scott Davidson, Cologne
Studio GOOD, Berlin
Dr Thomas Dirksen, Münster
Hendrik Dorgathen, Mülheim a. d. Ruhr
Dr Stefan Franken, Mülheim a. d. Ruhr
Hannes Wanderer, Peperoni-Books, Berlin
Jemma Conway, Barnsley
Richard King, Barnsley

Kulturstiftung der VG Bild-Kunst, Bonn

Hochschule Darmstadt, h_da

h_da
HOCHSCHULE DARMSTADT
UNIVERSITY OF APPLIED SCIENCES

About the Author

Photographer Michael Kerstgens was born in Llanelli, South Wales, in 1960. In 1965, he moved with his parents back to Mülheim an der Ruhr, Germany, where he grew up and went to school. He then studied Photography at the Folkwang University of the Arts (GHS) in Essen, Germany. He has worked as a freelance photographer since 1988.

From 1988 to 1991, he was also a partner of the Essen-based photo agency Antrazit. He received the Imke Folkerts Prize for Fine Art in 2005. The following year, he was awarded a working grant by VG Bild-Kunst and appointed to the German Photographic Association (DGPh).

In 2007, Michael Kerstgens became Professor of Documentary Photography at the Faculty of Design of h_da Darmstadt, University of Applied Sciences. His work *Neues Leben. Russen Juden Deutsche* (Kehrer Verlag, Heidelberg) on contemporary Jewish life in Germany was published in 2012.

He lives with his wife, Mariele Wirth, and their children, Paul, Robert, and Klara, in Oberhausen, Germany.

Imprint

First Edition, 2014

Copyright © 2014 Peperoni Books, Berlin
www.peperoni-books.de

Copyright © 2014 All Photographs & Texts
Michael Kerstgens, DGPh
www.kerstgens.de

Copy Editing/Translation
Scott Davidson, Cologne

Typesetting
Studio GOOD, Berlin
www.studio-good.de

Book Design
Michael Kerstgens

Production
Hannes Wanderer, Peperoni Books, Berlin

Printing
Wanderer Druck, Bad Münder

ISBN   978-3-941825-61-1